ignited Air Fryer Toaster Oven Cookbook for Beginners

600-Day Quick & Easy ignited Air Fryer Toaster Oven Recipes for Smart People on a Budget

Wenday Janes

Table of Contents

Introduction

We've "Packed a Punch" by adding these hand selected menu items for your devouring needs. Just putting in the food and turning on the machine. We've found that there are specific settings within the air fryer controls that make this device easy for anyone to cook up something delicious. Most of these recipes inside of this ignited Air Fryer Toaster Oven Cookbook are very healthy indeed! We always want to keep in account that there are a lot of families that want to eat as clean as they can and healthy.

With this book, you don't need to sacrifice flavor when trying to eat healthier. Many different basic and simple air fryer recipes are provided in this cookbook, so you can cook in your own kitchen easily, because these recipes will instruct you step by step, so that you can understand the process quickly.

Chapter 1: Breakfast

Strawberry Donuts

Preparation Time: 10 minutes
Cooking Time: 17 minutes
Serve: 12

Ingredients:

- 2 eggs
- ½ cup strawberries, chopped
- 1 tsp baking powder
- ¾ cup sugar
- ½ cup buttermilk
- ¼ cup olive oil
- 1 cup all-purpose flour
- ½ tsp vanilla
- ½ tsp salt

Directions:

1. Spray donut pan with cooking spray and set aside.
2. In a bowl, whisk eggs, vanilla, baking powder, sugar, buttermilk, oil, and salt until well combined.
3. Add flour and stir until well combined. Add strawberries and fold well.
4. Pour mixture into the prepared donut pan.
5. Place donut pan on a mesh rack. Insert the rack into the air fryer oven.
6. Set the temperature to 350 F and timer for 17 minutes. Press start.
7. Serve and enjoy.

Nutritional Value (Amount per Serving):

- Calories 138
- Fat 5.1 g
- Carbohydrates 21.7 g
- Sugar 13.4 g
- Protein 2.4 g
- Cholesterol 28 mg

Herb Egg Muffins

Preparation Time: 10 minutes
Cooking Time: 20 minutes
Serve: 6

Ingredients:

- 6 eggs
- 1/2 tbsp chives, chopped
- 1/2 tbsp fresh basil, chopped
- 1/4 cup mozzarella cheese, grated
- 1/2 tbsp fresh dill, chopped
- Pepper
- Salt

Directions:

1. In a bowl, whisk eggs with pepper and salt.
2. Add remaining ingredients and whisk well.
3. Pour egg mixture into the six silicone muffin molds.
4. Place muffins molds on a mesh rack. Insert the rack into the air fryer oven.
5. Set the temperature to 350 F and timer for 20 minutes. Press start.
6. Serve and enjoy.

Nutritional Value (Amount per Serving):

- Calories 65
- Fat 4.6 g
- Carbohydrates 0.6 g
- Sugar 0.4 g
- Protein 6 g
- Cholesterol 164 mg

Delicious Gruyere Cheese Bacon Egg Bite

Preparation Time: 10 minutes
Cooking Time: 5 minutes
Serve: 7

Ingredients:

- 4 eggs
- 1/2 cup cottage cheese, crumbled
- 1/2 cup gruyere cheese, shredded
- 1/4 cup bacon, cooked and crumbled

Directions:

1. Spray silicone muffin molds with cooking spray and set aside.
2. In a bowl, beat eggs until frothy. Add remaining ingredients and stir well.
3. Pour egg mixture into the prepared molds.
4. Place molds on mesh rack and insert into the air fryer oven.
5. Set the temperature to 330 F for 5 minutes. Press start.
6. Serve and enjoy.

Nutritional Value (Amount per Serving):

- Calories 85
- Fat 5.6 g
- Carbohydrates 0.8 g
- Sugar 0.3 g
- Protein 7.9 g
- Cholesterol 104 mg

Breakfast Cheese Egg Bake

Preparation Time: 10 minutes
Cooking Time: 25 minutes
Serve: 3

Ingredients:

- 6 eggs
- 1/4 lb parmesan cheese, grated
- 1/2 cup milk
- 1/4 tsp dry mustard
- 2 tbsp butter, melted
- Pepper
- Salt

Directions:

1. Spray a baking dish with cooking spray and set aside.
2. In a bowl, whisk eggs with milk, mustard, pepper, and salt. Stir in cheese.
3. Pour egg mixture into the prepared baking dish.
4. Place baking dish on mesh rack and insert into the air fryer oven.
5. Set the temperature to 350 F and timer for 25 minutes. Press start.
6. Serve and enjoy.

Nutritional Value (Amount per Serving):

- Calories 365
- Fat 29.9 g
- Carbohydrates 3.3 g
- Sugar 2.7 g
- Protein 22 g
- Cholesterol 391 mg

Baked Omelet

Preparation Time: 5 minutes
Cooking Time: 9 minutes
Serve: 1

Ingredients:

- 2 eggs, lightly beaten
- ¼ cup milk
- ¼ cup cheddar cheese, shredded
- Pepper
- Salt

Directions:

1. In a bowl, whisk eggs with milk, pepper, and salt.
2. Spray a small baking pan with cooking spray.
3. Pour egg mixture into the prepared pan.
4. Place baking pan on a mesh rack. Insert the rack into the air fryer oven.
5. Set the temperature to 350 F and timer for 6 minutes. Press start.
6. Sprinkle cheese on top and bake for 3 minutes more.
7. Serve and enjoy.

Nutritional Value (Amount per Serving):

- Calories 271
- Fat 19.4 g
- Carbohydrates 4.1 g
- Sugar 3.6 g
- Protein 20.1 g
- Cholesterol 362 mg

Cheesy Breakfast Quiche

Preparation Time: 10 minutes
Cooking Time: 45 minutes
Serve: 6

Ingredients:

- 6 eggs
- 1 cup cheddar cheese, grated
- 1 tsp garlic powder
- 1 cup milk
- 1 cup tomatoes, chopped
- Pepper
- Salt

Directions:

1. In a bowl, whisk eggs with cheese, milk, garlic powder, pepper, and salt. Stir in tomatoes.
2. Pour egg mixture into the greased pie dish.
3. Place dish on mesh rack then insert rack into the air fryer oven.
4. Set the temperature to 350 F for 45 minutes. Press start.
5. Serve and enjoy.

Nutritional Value (Amount per Serving):

- Calories 152
- Fat 11.3 g
- Carbohydrates 2.4 g
- Sugar 1.3 g
- Protein 10.7 g
- Cholesterol 183 mg

Healthy Oatmeal Muffins

Preparation Time: 10 minutes
Cooking Time: 30 minutes
Serve: 12

Ingredients:

- 3 cups old fashioned oats
- 1 tsp baking powder
- 1/4 cup maple syrup
- 1 1/4 cups applesauce
- 1 1/2 cups milk
- 1 cup apples, chopped
- 1/2 tsp vanilla
- 1 1/2 tsp cinnamon
- 1/4 tsp salt

Directions:

1. Line the muffin pan with cupcake liners and set aside.
2. Add all ingredients except for the apples in a large bowl and mix until well combined. Add apples and stir well.
3. Pour batter into the prepared muffin pan.
4. Place muffin pan on a mesh rack. Insert the rack into the air fryer oven.
5. Set the temperature to 350 F and timer for 30 minutes. Press start.
6. Serve and enjoy.

Nutritional Value (Amount per Serving):

- Calories 210
- Fat 3.3 g
- Carbohydrates 38.6 g
- Sugar 10.9 g
- Protein 6.1 g
- Cholesterol 3 mg

Spicy Egg Bite

Preparation Time: 10 minutes
Cooking Time: 5 minutes
Serve: 7

Ingredients:

- 4 eggs
- 1/2 cup cottage cheese, crumbled
- 1/2 cup pepper jack cheese, shredded
- 1/4 cup green chilis, diced
- Pepper
- Salt

Directions:

1. Spray silicone muffin mold with cooking spray and set aside.
2. In a bowl, beat eggs until frothy. Add remaining ingredients and stir to well.
3. Pour egg mixture into the prepared molds.
4. Place molds on mesh rack and insert into the air fryer oven.
5. Set the temperature to 330 F for 5 minutes. Press start.
6. Serve and enjoy.

Nutritional Value (Amount per Serving):

- Calories 55
- Fat 3.1 g
- Carbohydrates 1.4 g
- Sugar 0.5 g
- Protein 5.5 g
- Cholesterol 96 mg

Healthy Zucchini Frittata

Preparation Time: 10 minutes
Cooking Time: 30 minutes
Serve: 4

Ingredients:

- 8 eggs
- 2 zucchini, chopped and cooked
- 1 tsp garlic powder
- 3 tbsp parmesan cheese, grated
- Pepper
- Salt

Directions:

1. In a large bowl, whisk eggs with garlic powder, pepper, and salt. Stir in cheese, and zucchini.
2. Pour egg mixture into the greased baking dish.
3. Place dish on mesh rack then insert rack into the air fryer oven.
4. Set the temperature to 350 F for 30 minutes. Press start.
5. Serve and enjoy.

Nutritional Value (Amount per Serving):

- Calories 155
- Fat 9.9 g
- Carbohydrates 4.7 g
- Sugar 2.6 g
- Protein 13.8 g
- Cholesterol 330 mg

Baked Breakfast Donuts

Preparation Time: 10 minutes
Cooking Time: 20 minutes
Serve: 6

Ingredients:

- 4 eggs
- 3 tbsp cocoa powder
- 1/4 cup butter, melted
- 1/3 cup coconut flour
- 1/2 tsp baking soda
- 1/2 tsp baking powder
- 1/2 tsp instant coffee
- 1/3 cup milk
- 1 tbsp liquid stevia

Directions:

1. Add all ingredients into the large bowl and mix until well combined.
2. Pour batter into the silicone donut molds.
3. Place donut molds on a mesh rack. Insert the rack into the air fryer oven.
4. Set the temperature to 350 F and timer for 20 minutes. Press start.
5. Serve and enjoy.

Nutritional Value (Amount per Serving):

- Calories 146
- Fat 12 g
- Carbohydrates 5.6 g
- Sugar 0.7 g
- Protein 5.2 g
- Cholesterol 129 mg

Chapter 2: Poultry

Easy & Tasty Chicken Wings

Preparation Time: 10 minutes
Cooking Time: 30 minutes
Serve: 2

Ingredients:

- 1 lb chicken wings
- 1/4 cup honey
- 1/2 lime juice
- 1 tbsp butter
- 1 1/2 tbsp soy sauce
- 2 tbsp sriracha sauce

Directions:

1. Place chicken wings on mesh rack then insert rack into the air fryer oven.
2. Select air fry mode then set the temperature to 360 F and timer for 30 minutes. Press start. Turn chicken wings halfway through.
3. Meanwhile, add the remaining ingredients into the saucepan and bring to boil for 3 minutes.
4. Once wings are done then toss them in a sauce.
5. Serve and enjoy.

Nutritional Value (Amount per Serving):

- Calories 721
- Fat 32.6 g
- Carbohydrates 37.8 g
- Sugar 36.2 g
- Protein 66.6 g
- Cholesterol 227 mg

Southwest Chicken

Preparation Time: 10 minutes
Cooking Time: 25 minutes
Serve: 2

Ingredients:

- 1/2 lb chicken breasts, skinless and boneless
- 1 tbsp lime juice
- 1/8 tsp garlic powder
- 1/8 tsp onion powder
- 1/4 tsp chili powder
- 1/2 tbsp olive oil
- 1/4 tsp cumin
- 1/8 tsp salt

Directions:

1. Add all ingredients into the zip-lock bag and shake well and place it in the fridge for 1 hour.
2. Place marinated chicken on parchment-lined mesh rack then insert rack into the air fryer oven.
3. Select air fry mode then set the temperature to 400 F and timer for 25 minutes. Press start.
4. Turn chicken halfway through.
5. Serve and enjoy.

Nutritional Value (Amount per Serving):

- Calories 255
- Fat 12 g
- Carbohydrates 2.4 g
- Sugar 0.5 g
- Protein 33 g
- Cholesterol 101 mg

Lemon Garlic Chicken

Preparation Time: 10 minutes
Cooking Time: 30 minutes
Serve: 4

Ingredients:

- 1 lb chicken drumsticks
- 4 garlic cloves, minced
- 1 tbsp olive oil
- 1 tbsp parsley, minced
- 1/2 fresh lemon juice
- Pepper
- Salt

Directions:

1. Season chicken with pepper and salt.
2. Mix together parsley, lemon juice, garlic, and oil and rub over chicken.
3. Place chicken drumsticks on mesh rack then insert rack into the air fryer oven.
4. Set the temperature to 380 F and timer for 30 minutes. Press start. Turn chicken halfway through.
5. Serve and enjoy.

Nutritional Value (Amount per Serving):

- Calories 225
- Fat 10.1 g
- Carbohydrates 1.2 g
- Sugar 0.2 g
- Protein 31.5 g
- Cholesterol 100 mg

Delicious Mustard Chicken

Preparation Time: 10 minutes
Cooking Time: 20 minutes
Serve: 4

Ingredients:

- 1 lbs chicken tenders
- 1/2 cup whole grain mustard
- 1/2 tsp paprika
- 1/2 tsp pepper
- 1 garlic clove, minced
- 1/2 oz fresh lemon juice
- 2 tbsp fresh tarragon, chopped
- 1/4 tsp kosher salt

Directions:

1. Add all ingredients except chicken to the large bowl and mix well.
2. Add chicken to the bowl and stir until well coated.
3. Place chicken tenders on mesh rack then insert rack into the air fryer oven.
4. Set the temperature to 380 F and timer for 20 minutes. Press start. Turn chicken halfway through.
5. Serve and enjoy.

Nutritional Value (Amount per Serving):

- Calories 245
- Fat 9.5 g
- Carbohydrates 3.1 g
- Sugar 0.1 g
- Protein 33.2 g
- Cholesterol 101 mg

Honey Chicken Drumsticks

Preparation Time: 10 minutes
Cooking Time: 12 minutes
Serve: 2

Ingredients:

- 2 chicken drumsticks
- 1 tsp honey
- 1/2 tsp mustard
- 1/2 tbsp olive oil
- 1/2 tsp garlic paste
- Pepper
- Salt

Directions:

1. Add all ingredients to the large bowl and mix well.
2. Place chicken drumsticks on mesh rack then insert rack into the air fryer oven.
3. Select air fry mode then set the temperature to 350 F and timer for 12 minutes. Press start.
4. Turn chicken halfway through.
5. Serve and enjoy.

Nutritional Value (Amount per Serving):

- Calories 125
- Fat 6.4 g
- Carbohydrates 3.4 g
- Sugar 2.9 g
- Protein 12.9 g
- Cholesterol 40 mg

Crispy Chicken Wings

Preparation Time: 10 minutes
Cooking Time: 25 minutes
Serve: 4

Ingredients:

- 1 lb chicken wings
- 1/4 cup parmesan cheese, grated
- 1/2 tbsp garlic powder
- 1/2 tsp onion powder
- 2 tbsp cornstarch
- 1/2 tsp paprika
- Pepper
- Salt

Directions:

1. In a bowl, mix together cornstarch, garlic powder, onion powder, paprika, parmesan cheese, pepper, and salt.
2. Add chicken wings in cornstarch mixture and toss until well coated.
3. Place chicken wings on mesh rack then insert rack into the air fryer oven.
4. Select air fry mode then set the temperature to 380 F and timer for 25 minutes. Press start. Turn chicken wings halfway through.
5. Serve and enjoy.

Nutritional Value (Amount per Serving):

- Calories 255
- Fat 9.7 g
- Carbohydrates 5 g
- Sugar 0.4 g
- Protein 34.9 g
- Cholesterol 105 mg

Spicy Chicken Wings

Preparation Time: 10 minutes
Cooking Time: 30 minutes
Serve: 4

Ingredients:

- 2 lbs chicken wings
- ½ tsp smoked paprika
- 2 tsp garlic powder
- 4 tsp chili powder
- 3 tbsp olive oil
- Pepper
- Salt

Directions:

1. Add chicken wings and remaining ingredients into the zip-lock bag and shake well to coat.
2. Place chicken wings on mesh rack then insert rack into the air fryer oven.
3. Select air fry mode then set the temperature to 380 F and timer for 30 minutes. Press start. Turn chicken wings halfway through.
4. Serve and enjoy.

Nutritional Value (Amount per Serving):

- Calories 535
- Fat 27.8 g
- Carbohydrates 2.5 g
- Sugar 0.5 g
- Protein 66.2 g
- Cholesterol 202 mg

Crispy Chicken

Preparation Time: 10 minutes
Cooking Time: 14 minutes
Serve: 2

Ingredients:

- 2 chicken breasts, boneless and skinless
- 2 cups crushed crackers
- 1 tbsp olive oil
- Pepper
- Salt

Directions:

1. Season chicken with pepper and salt.
2. Brush chicken with oil and coat with crushed crackers.
3. Place chicken on mesh rack then insert rack into the air fryer oven.
4. Set the temperature to 370 F and timer for 14 minutes. Press start. Turn chicken halfway through.
5. Serve and enjoy.

Nutritional Value (Amount per Serving):

- Calories 280
- Fat 14.2 g
- Carbohydrates 0.7 g
- Sugar 0 g
- Protein 33 g
- Cholesterol 116 mg

Herb Chicken Wings

Preparation Time: 10 minutes
Cooking Time: 15 minutes
Serve: 4

Ingredients:

- 2 lbs chicken wings
- 1/2 cup parmesan cheese, grated
- 1 tsp Herb de Provence
- 1 tsp smoked paprika
- Pepper
- Salt

Directions:

1. Add cheese, paprika, herb de Provence, pepper, and salt into the large mixing bowl. Add chicken wings into the bowl and toss well to coat.
2. Place chicken wings on mesh rack then insert rack into the air fryer oven.
3. Select air fry mode then set the temperature to 350 F and timer for 15 minutes. Press start. Turn chicken wings halfway through.
4. Serve and enjoy.

Nutritional Value (Amount per Serving):

- Calories 475
- Fat 19.6 g
- Carbohydrates 0.8 g
- Sugar 0.1 g
- Protein 69.7 g
- Cholesterol 211 mg

Turkey Patties

Preparation Time: 10 minutes
Cooking Time: 20 minutes
Serve: 4

Ingredients:

- 1 lb ground turkey
- 1 tbsp olive oil
- 1 tbsp garlic, minced
- 4 oz feta cheese, crumbled
- 1 1/2 cups fresh spinach, chopped
- 1 tsp Italian seasoning
- Pepper
- Salt

Directions:

1. Add ground turkey and remaining ingredients into the mixing bowl and mix until well combined.
2. Make four patties from the turkey mixture and place on mesh rack then insert rack into the air fryer oven.
3. Set the temperature to 400 F and timer for 20 minutes. Press start.
4. Serve and enjoy.

Nutritional Value (Amount per Serving):

- Calories 335
- Fat 22.4 g
- Carbohydrates 2.4 g
- Sugar 1.3 g
- Protein 35.5 g
- Cholesterol 142 mg

Perfect Chicken Tenders

Preparation Time: 10 minutes
Cooking Time: 13 minutes
Serve: 4

Ingredients:

- 6 chicken tenders
- 1 tsp paprika
- 1 tsp onion powder
- 1 tsp oregano
- 1 tsp garlic powder
- 1 tsp kosher salt

Directions:

1. In a small bowl, mix together onion powder, oregano, garlic powder, paprika, and salt and rub all over chicken tenders.
2. Spray chicken tenders with cooking spray.
3. Place chicken tenders on mesh rack then insert rack into the air fryer oven.
4. Select air fry mode then set the temperature to 380 F and timer for 13 minutes. Press start. Turn chicken halfway through.
5. Serve and enjoy.

Nutritional Value (Amount per Serving):

- Calories 425
- Fat 16.4 g
- Carbohydrates 1.5 g
- Sugar 0.5 g
- Protein 63.7 g
- Cholesterol 195 mg

Chicken Meatballs

Preparation Time: 10 minutes
Cooking Time: 12 minutes
Serve: 4

Ingredients:

- 1 egg, lightly beaten
- 1/2 lb ground chicken
- 2 garlic cloves, minced
- 1/2 cup swiss cheese, shredded
- 1/3 cup onion, diced
- 1/2 lb ham, diced
- Pepper
- Salt

Directions:

1. Add all ingredients into the mixing bowl and mix until well combined. Place in refrigerator for 30 minutes.
2. Make balls from mixture and place on mesh rack then insert rack into the air fryer oven.
3. Select air fry mode then set the temperature to 390 F and timer for 12 minutes. Press start.
4. Serve and enjoy.

Nutritional Value (Amount per Serving):

- Calories 275
- Fat 13.9 g
- Carbohydrates 4.4 g
- Sugar 0.7 g
- Protein 31 g
- Cholesterol 136 mg

Meatballs

Preparation Time: 10 minutes
Cooking Time: 10 minutes
Serve: 4

Ingredients:

- 1 lb ground chicken
- 2 tbsp parmesan cheese, grated
- 1/4 cup sun-dried tomatoes, drained
- 2 tsp garlic, minced
- 3/4 cup almond flour
- 1/4 cup feta cheese, crumbled
- 3 cups baby spinach
- Pepper
- Salt

Directions:

1. Add spinach, sun-dried tomatoes, and 1 tsp garlic into the food processor and process until a paste is formed.
2. Add spinach mixture into the large mixing bowl. Add remaining ingredients into the bowl and mix until well combined.
3. Make balls from mixture and place on mesh rack then insert rack into the air fryer oven.
4. Select air fry mode then set the temperature to 400 F and timer for 10 minutes. Press start.
5. Serve and enjoy.

Nutritional Value (Amount per Serving):

- Calories 305
- Fat 14.7 g
- Carbohydrates 3.5 g
- Sugar 1 g
- Protein 38.4 g
- Cholesterol 114 mg

Meatballs

Preparation Time: 10 minutes
Cooking Time: 10 minutes
Serve: 4

Ingredients:

- 1 egg, lightly beaten
- 1 bell pepper, chopped
- 1 1/2 lbs ground turkey
- 1 tbsp fresh cilantro, minced
- 4 tbsp fresh parsley, chopped
- Pepper
- Salt

Directions:

1. Add all ingredients into the mixing bowl and mix until well combined.
2. Make balls from mixture and place on mesh rack then insert rack into the air fryer oven.
3. Select air fry mode then set the temperature to 400 F and timer for 10 minutes. Press start.
4. Serve and enjoy.

Nutritional Value (Amount per Serving):

- Calories 360
- Fat 19.9 g
- Carbohydrates 2.6 g
- Sugar 1.6 g
- Protein 48.3 g
- Cholesterol 239 mg

Cajun Chicken

Preparation Time: 10 minutes
Cooking Time: 15 minutes
Serve: 4

Ingredients:

- 4 chicken thighs, boneless
- 1 tsp paprika
- 3 tbsp parmesan cheese, grated
- 1/3 cup almond flour
- 1/2 tsp cajun seasoning
- 1 tsp dried mixed herbs

Directions:

1. In a medium bowl, mix together almond flour, parmesan cheese, paprika, dried mixed herbs, and Cajun seasoning.
2. Spray chicken thighs with cooking spray and coat with almond flour mixture.
3. Place coated chicken thighs on mesh rack then insert rack into the air fryer oven.
4. Select air fry mode then set the temperature to 400 F and timer for 15 minutes. Press start. Turn chicken halfway through.
5. Serve and enjoy.

Nutritional Value (Amount per Serving):

- Calories 325
- Fat 14.3 g
- Carbohydrates 1.3 g
- Sugar 0.1 g
- Protein 46.2 g
- Cholesterol 137 mg

Chapter 3: Beef, Pork & Lamb

Tasty Pork Ribs

Preparation Time: 10 minutes
Cooking Time: 30 minutes
Serve: 8

Ingredients:

- 2 lbs pork ribs, boneless
- ½ tsp Italian seasoning
- 2 tbsp olive oil
- 1 tbsp onion powder
- 1 ½ tbsp garlic powder
- Pepper
- Salt

Directions:

1. In a small bowl, mix onion powder, garlic powder, Italian seasoning, pepper, and salt.
2. Brush pork ribs with oil and rub with spices mixture.
3. Place pork ribs on mesh rack then insert rack into the air fryer oven.
4. Set the temperature to 350 F and timer for 25-30 minutes. Press start.
5. Serve and enjoy.

Nutritional Value (Amount per Serving):

- Calories 320
- Fat 20.2 g
- Carbohydrates 1.9 g
- Sugar 0.7 g
- Protein 30.4 g
- Cholesterol 117 mg

Meatballs

Preparation Time: 10 minutes
Cooking Time: 20 minutes
Serve: 4

Ingredients:

- 1 egg, lightly beaten
- 1 lb ground lamb
- 1 tbsp garlic, minced
- 1/4 tsp pepper
- 1/4 tsp red pepper flakes
- 1 tsp ground cumin
- 2 tsp fresh oregano, chopped
- 2 tbsp fresh parsley, chopped
- 1 tsp kosher salt

Directions:

1. Add all ingredients into the mixing bowl and mix until well combined.
2. Make balls from the meat mixture and place on mesh rack then insert rack into the air fryer oven.
3. Set the temperature to 400 F and timer for 20-25 minutes. Press start.
4. Serve and enjoy.

Nutritional Value (Amount per Serving):

- Calories 325
- Fat 20.2 g
- Carbohydrates 1.7 g
- Sugar 0.2 g
- Protein 33.6 g
- Cholesterol 143 mg

Easy Lamb Patties

Preparation Time: 10 minutes
Cooking Time: 20 minutes
Serve: 6

Ingredients:

- 1 ½ lbs ground lamb
- 3 green onions, sliced
- 1 tbsp fresh ginger, grated
- Pepper
- Salt

Directions:

1. Add all ingredients into the mixing bowl and mix until well combined.
2. Make 6 patties from meat mixture and place on mesh rack then insert rack into the air fryer oven.
3. Set the temperature to 375 F and timer for 20 minutes. Press start.
4. Serve and enjoy.

Nutritional Value (Amount per Serving):

- Calories 215
- Fat 8.4 g
- Carbohydrates 1.2 g
- Sugar 0.2 g
- Protein 32.1 g
- Cholesterol 102 mg

Lamb Cutlets

Preparation Time: 10 minutes
Cooking Time: 30 minutes
Serve: 4

Ingredients:

- 4 lamb cutlets
- 1 tsp olive oil
- 1/2 tbsp chives, chopped
- 2 tbsp mustard
- 2 garlic cloves, minced
- 1/2 tbsp oregano, chopped
- 1/2 tbsp basil, chopped
- Pepper
- Salt

Directions:

1. Add lamb cutlets and remaining ingredients to the mixing bowl and coat well.
2. Place lamb cutlets on mesh rack then insert rack into the air fryer oven.
3. Select air fry mode then set the temperature to 380 F and timer for 30 minutes. Press start. Flip lamb cutlets halfway through.
4. Serve and enjoy.

Nutritional Value (Amount per Serving):

- Calories 201
- Fat 9.1 g
- Carbohydrates 3 g
- Sugar 0.4 g
- Protein 25.5 g
- Cholesterol 77 mg

Herb Pork Chops

Preparation Time: 10 minutes
Cooking Time: 25 minutes
Serve: 4

Ingredients:

- 4 pork chops, boneless and cut 1/2-inch thick
- 1 tsp dried rosemary, crushed
- ¼ tsp dried thyme, crushed
- 1 tbsp olive oil
- 1/4 tsp pepper
- 1/4 tsp salt

Directions:

1. Season pork chops with pepper and salt.
2. Mix rosemary, thyme, and oil and rub all over pork chops.
3. Place pork chops on mesh rack then insert rack into the air fryer oven.
4. Set the temperature to 350 F and timer for 25 minutes. Press start.
5. Serve and enjoy.

Nutritional Value (Amount per Serving):

- Calories 257
- Fat 19.9 g
- Carbohydrates 0.3 g
- Sugar 0 g
- Protein 18 g
- Cholesterol 69 mg

Easy Ranch Pork Chops

Preparation Time: 10 minutes
Cooking Time: 35 minutes
Serve: 6

Ingredients:

- 6 pork chops, boneless
- 2 tbsp olive oil
- 1 oz ranch seasoning

Directions:

1. Mix oil and ranch seasoning and rub over pork chops.
2. Place pork chops on mesh rack then insert rack into the air fryer oven.
3. Select air fry mode then set the temperature to 400 F and timer for 35 minutes. Press start. Turn pork chops halfway through.
4. Serve and enjoy.

Nutritional Value (Amount per Serving):

- Calories 311
- Fat 24.6 g
- Carbohydrates 0 g
- Sugar 0 g
- Protein 18 g
- Cholesterol 69 mg

Healthy & Juicy Pork Chops

Preparation Time: 5 minutes
Cooking Time: 16 minutes
Serve: 4

Ingredients:

- 4 pork chops, boneless
- 1/2 tsp onion powder
- 1/2 tsp garlic powder
- 1/4 tsp sugar
- 2 tsp olive oil
- 1/2 tsp celery seed
- 1/2 tsp parsley
- 1/2 tsp salt

Directions:

1. In a small bowl, mix sugar, garlic powder, onion powder, parsley, celery seed, and salt.
2. Rub oil and seasoning on the pork chops.
3. Place pork chops on mesh rack then insert rack into the air fryer oven.
4. Set the temperature to 350 F and timer for 16 minutes. Press start.
5. Serve and enjoy.

Nutritional Value (Amount per Serving):

- Calories 280
- Fat 22.3 g
- Carbohydrates 0.9 g
- Sugar 0.5 g
- Protein 18.1 g
- Cholesterol 69 mg

Meatballs

Preparation Time: 10 minutes
Cooking Time: 35 minutes
Serve: 4

Ingredients:

- 1 lb ground beef
- 1/3 cup milk
- 2 jalapenos, minced
- 4 oz cream cheese
- 1 tsp dried basil
- 2 tbsp Worcestershire sauce
- 1/2 cup cheddar cheese, shredded
- 3/4 cup breadcrumbs
- 1/2 onion, minced
- 1 tsp salt

Directions:

1. Add all ingredients into the bowl and mix until well combined.
2. Make balls from the meat mixture and place on mesh rack then insert rack into the air fryer oven.
3. Set the temperature to 400 F and timer for 35 minutes. Press start.
4. Serve and enjoy.

Nutritional Value (Amount per Serving):

- Calories 476
- Fat 23.2 g
- Carbohydrates 19.7 g
- Sugar 4.6 g
- Protein 43.7 g
- Cholesterol 149 mg

Tasty Pork Patties

Preparation Time: 10 minutes
Cooking Time: 30 minutes
Serve: 6

Ingredients:

- 1 egg
- 2 ¼ lbs ground pork
- 1 onion, minced
- 1 carrot, minced
- ½ tsp pepper
- ½ cup breadcrumbs
- 1 tsp garlic powder
- 1 tsp paprika
- 1 tsp salt

Directions:

1. Add all ingredients into the mixing bowl and mix until well combined.
2. Make six patties from mixture and place on mesh rack then insert rack into the air fryer oven.
3. Set the temperature to 375 F and timer for 25-35 minutes. Press start.
4. Serve and enjoy.

Nutritional Value (Amount per Serving):

- Calories 305
- Fat 7.3 g
- Carbohydrates 9.9 g
- Sugar 2.1 g
- Protein 47.1 g
- Cholesterol 151 mg

Healthy Beef Patties

Preparation Time: 10 minutes
Cooking Time: 35 minutes
Serve: 6

Ingredients:

- 1 lb ground beef
- 2 eggs, lightly beaten
- 1/2 tsp chili powder
- 1 tsp curry powder
- 1 cup breadcrumbs
- 1/2 onion, chopped
- 2 medium zucchini, grated
- Pepper
- Salt

Directions:

1. Add all ingredients into the large bowl and mix until well combined.
2. Make patties from meat mixture and place on mesh rack then insert rack into the air fryer oven.
3. Set the temperature to 400 F and timer for 35 minutes. Press start.
4. Serve and enjoy.

Nutritional Value (Amount per Serving):

- Calories 245
- Fat 7.3 g
- Carbohydrates 16.4 g
- Sugar 2.8 g
- Protein 28.1 g
- Cholesterol 122 mg

Creole Chops

Preparation Time: 10 minutes
Cooking Time: 12 minutes
Serve: 6

Ingredients:

- 1 1/2 lbs pork chops, boneless
- 1 tsp paprika
- 1 tsp Creole seasoning
- 1 tsp garlic powder
- 1/4 cup parmesan cheese, grated
- 1/3 cup almond flour

Directions:

1. Add all ingredients except pork chops into the zip-lock bag.
2. Add pork chops into the bag. Seal bag and shake well.
3. Remove pork chops from the zip-lock bag and place on mesh rack then insert rack into the air fryer oven.
4. Select air fry mode then set the temperature to 360 F and timer for 12 minutes. Press start.
5. Serve and enjoy.

Nutritional Value (Amount per Serving):

- Calories 416
- Fat 32 g
- Carbohydrates 2 g
- Sugar 0.2 g
- Protein 28.2 g
- Cholesterol 100 mg

Spiced Pork Chops

Preparation Time: 10 minutes
Cooking Time: 20 minutes
Serve: 4

Ingredients:

- 4 pork chops, boneless
- 2 tbsp olive oil
- For the dry rub:
- ½ tsp garlic powder
- 2 tbsp brown sugar
- 1 tsp smoked paprika
- ¼ tsp pepper
- ½ tsp Italian seasoning
- ½ tsp sea salt

Directions:

1. Brush pork chops with olive oil.
2. In a small bowl, mix together all rub ingredients and rub all over pork chops.
3. Place pork chops on mesh rack then insert rack into the air fryer oven.
4. Set the temperature to 375 F and timer for 20-25 minutes. Press start.
5. Serve and enjoy.

Nutritional Value (Amount per Serving):

- Calories 335
- Fat 27.1 g
- Carbohydrates 5.1 g
- Sugar 4.6 g
- Protein 18.1 g
- Cholesterol 69 mg

Beef Fajitas

Preparation Time: 10 minutes
Cooking Time: 8 minutes
Serve: 4

Ingredients:

- 1 lb steak, sliced
- 1 tsp cumin
- 1 yellow bell peppers, sliced
- 1/2 tbsp chili powder
- 3 tbsp olive oil
- 1 green bell peppers, sliced
- 1 tsp garlic powder
- 1 tsp smoked paprika
- Pepper
- Salt

Directions:

1. In a large bowl, toss sliced steak with remaining ingredients and spread on mesh rack then insert rack into the air fryer oven.
2. Select air fry mode then set the temperature to 390 F and timer for 8 minutes. Press start.
3. Serve and enjoy.

Nutritional Value (Amount per Serving):

- Calories 346
- Fat 16.7 g
- Carbohydrates 6.1 g
- Sugar 3 g
- Protein 42 g
- Cholesterol 102 mg

Garlic Lemon Lamb Chops

Preparation Time: 10 minutes
Cooking Time: 6 minutes
Serve: 6

Ingredients:

- 6 lamb loin chops
- 1 tbsp dried rosemary
- 1 tbsp olive oil
- 1 tbsp garlic, minced
- 2 tbsp fresh lemon juice
- 1 ½ tbsp lemon zest
- Pepper
- Salt

Directions:

1. Add lamb chops in a mixing bowl.
2. Add remaining ingredients on top of lamb chops and coat well.
3. Arrange lamb chops on mesh rack then insert rack into the air fryer oven.
4. Select air fry mode then set the temperature to 400 F and timer for 6 minutes. Press start.
5. Serve and enjoy.

Nutritional Value (Amount per Serving):

- Calories 70
- Fat 6 g
- Carbohydrates 1.2 g
- Sugar 0.2 g
- Protein 3 g
- Cholesterol 0 mg

BBQ Pork Chops

Preparation Time: 10 minutes
Cooking Time: 14 minutes
Serve: 2

Ingredients:

- 2 pork chops
- 1/4 cup BBQ sauce
- 1 tsp garlic, minced
- 1/2 tsp olive oil
- Pepper
- Salt

Directions:

1. Add all ingredients into the bowl and mix well and place in the refrigerator for 1 hour.
2. Place marinated pork chops on mesh rack then insert rack into the air fryer oven.
3. Select air fry mode then set the temperature to 350 F and timer for 14 minutes. Press start. Turn pork chops halfway through.
4. Serve and enjoy.

Nutritional Value (Amount per Serving):

- Calories 315
- Fat 21.1 g
- Carbohydrates 12.4 g
- Sugar 8.2 g
- Protein 18.2 g
- Cholesterol 69 mg

Chapter 4: Fish & Seafood

Tasty Garlic Butter Shrimp

Preparation Time: 10 minutes
Cooking Time: 10 minutes
Serve: 4

Ingredients:

- 1 lb shrimp, peeled and deveined
- 1/4 cup butter, melted
- 4 tbsp garlic, minced
- 2 tbsp olive oil
- Pepper
- Salt

Directions:

1. Add shrimp into the mixing bowl.
2. Add remaining ingredients and toss well.
3. Add shrimp on mesh rack then insert rack into the air fryer oven.
4. Select air fry mode then set the temperature to 400 F and timer for 10 minutes. Press start.
5. Serve and enjoy.

Nutritional Value (Amount per Serving):

- Calories 309
- Fat 20.5 g
- Carbohydrates 4.5 g
- Sugar 0.1 g
- Protein 26.5 g
- Cholesterol 269 mg

Shrimp Fajitas

Preparation Time: 10 minutes
Cooking Time: 22 minutes
Serve: 12

Ingredients:

- 1 lb shrimp, tail-off
- 1 red bell pepper, diced
- 2 tbsp taco seasoning
- 1/2 cup onion, diced
- 1 green bell pepper, diced

Directions:

1. Add shrimp, taco seasoning, onion, and bell peppers into the mixing bowl and toss well.
2. Place shrimp mixture on mesh rack then insert rack into the air fryer oven.
3. Select air fry mode then set the temperature to 390 F and timer for 22 minutes. Press start. Stir halfway through.
4. Serve and enjoy.

Nutritional Value (Amount per Serving):

- Calories 55
- Fat 0.8 g
- Carbohydrates 2.7 g
- Sugar 1.2 g
- Protein 9 g
- Cholesterol 80 mg

Herb Lemon Salmon

Preparation Time: 10 minutes
Cooking Time: 10 minutes
Serve: 2

Ingredients:

- 2 salmon fillets
- 1 tsp garlic, minced
- 1 tbsp thyme, diced
- 1 tbsp parsley, diced
- 2 tsp lime zest
- 2 tsp lemon zest
- 1 tbsp olive oil
- Pepper
- Salt

Directions:

1. In a small bowl, mix together lime zest, lemon zest, oil, garlic, thyme, parsley, pepper, and salt and rub over salmon.
2. Place salmon fillets on mesh rack then insert rack into the air fryer oven.
3. Select air fry mode then set the temperature to 400 F and timer for 10 minutes. Press start.
4. Serve and enjoy.

Nutritional Value (Amount per Serving):

- Calories 305
- Fat 18.1 g
- Carbohydrates 2.2 g
- Sugar 0.2 g
- Protein 34.9 g
- Cholesterol 78 mg

Crab Patties

Preparation Time: 10 minutes
Cooking Time: 15 minutes
Serve: 4

Ingredients:

- 1 egg, lightly beaten
- 2 tbsp parsley, chopped
- 1 tsp old bay seasoning
- 1 tsp Worcestershire sauce
- 1/2 tsp Dijon mustard
- 1/2 cup breadcrumbs
- 1 cup crushed crackers
- 1 cup crab meat
- 1 onion, chopped
- 2 tbsp mayonnaise
- 1/2 tsp salt

Directions:

1. Add all ingredients into the mixing bowl and mix until well combined.
2. Make patties from mixture and place on mesh rack then insert rack into the air fryer oven.
3. Select air fry mode then set the temperature to 350 F and timer for 15 minutes. Press start. Turn patties halfway through.
4. Serve and enjoy.

Nutritional Value (Amount per Serving):

- Calories 145
- Fat 6 g
- Carbohydrates 18.4 g
- Sugar 3.6 g
- Protein 5 g
- Cholesterol 47 mg

Healthy Salmon Patties

Preparation Time: 10 minutes
Cooking Time: 10 minutes
Serve: 4

Ingredients:

- 15 oz can salmon, drained and remove bones
- 1/4 cup onion, chopped
- 1 egg, lightly beaten
- 1 tsp dill, chopped
- 1/2 cup breadcrumbs
- Pepper
- Salt

Directions:

1. Add all ingredients into the mixing bowl and mix until well combined.
2. Make patties from mixture and place on mesh rack then insert rack into the air fryer oven.
3. Select air fry mode then set the temperature to 370 F and timer for 10 minutes. Press start. Turn patties halfway through.
4. Serve and enjoy.

Nutritional Value (Amount per Serving):

- Calories 221
- Fat 8.3 g
- Carbohydrates 10.6 g
- Sugar 1.2 g
- Protein 24.3 g
- Cholesterol 99 mg

Spicy Scallops

Preparation Time: 10 minutes
Cooking Time: 4 minutes
Serve: 2

Ingredients:

- 8 scallops
- 1 tbsp olive oil
- ¼ tsp cayenne
- Pepper
- Salt

Directions:

1. Brush scallops with oil and season with cayenne, pepper, and salt.
2. Place scallops on mesh rack then insert rack into the air fryer oven.
3. Select air fry mode then set the temperature to 390 F and timer for 4 minutes. Press start.
4. Serve and enjoy.

Nutritional Value (Amount per Serving):

- Calories 165
- Fat 7.9 g
- Carbohydrates 2.9 g
- Sugar 0 g
- Protein 20.2 g
- Cholesterol 40 mg

Garlic Butter Salmon

Preparation Time: 10 minutes
Cooking Time: 7 minutes
Serve: 4

Ingredients:

- 1 lb salmon fillets
- 1/4 cup parmesan cheese, grated
- 1/4 cup butter, melted
- 2 tbsp parsley, chopped
- 2 tbsp garlic, minced
- Pepper
- Salt

Directions:

1. Season salmon with pepper and salt.
2. In a small bowl, mix together butter, cheese, garlic, and parsley and brush over salmon fillets.
3. Place salmon fillets on mesh rack then insert rack into the air fryer oven.
4. Select air fry mode then set the temperature to 400 F and timer for 7 minutes. Press start.
5. Serve and enjoy.

Nutritional Value (Amount per Serving):

- Calories 275
- Fat 19.8 g
- Carbohydrates 1.7 g
- Sugar 0.1 g
- Protein 24.3 g
- Cholesterol 85 mg

Juicy Baked Cod

Preparation Time: 10 minutes
Cooking Time: 10 minutes
Serve: 2

Ingredients:

- 1 lb cod fillets
- 1 tbsp lemon juice
- 1 1/2 tbsp olive oil
- 3 dashes cayenne pepper
- 1/4 tsp salt

Directions:

1. In a small bowl, mix together olive oil, cayenne pepper, lemon juice, and salt.
2. Brush fish fillets with oil mixture.
3. Place fish fillets on mesh rack then insert rack into the air fryer oven.
4. Set the temperature to 400 F and timer for 10 minutes. Press start.
5. Serve and enjoy.

Nutritional Value (Amount per Serving):

- Calories 275
- Fat 12.7 g
- Carbohydrates 0.4 g
- Sugar 0.2 g
- Protein 40.6 g
- Cholesterol 111 mg

Tuna Steaks

Preparation Time: 10 minutes
Cooking Time: 4 minutes
Serve: 2

Ingredients:

- 12 tuna steaks, skinless and boneless
- 1 tsp ginger, grated
- 4 tbsp soy sauce
- 1/2 tsp rice vinegar
- 1 tsp sesame oil

Directions:

1. Add tuna steaks and remaining ingredients in the zip-lock bag. Seal bag and place in the refrigerator for 30 minutes.
2. Place tuna steaks on mesh rack then insert rack into the air fryer oven.
3. Select air fry mode then set the temperature to 380 F and timer for 4 minutes. Press start.
4. Serve and enjoy.

Nutritional Value (Amount per Serving):

- Calories 981
- Fat 34.4 g
- Carbohydrates 3.1 g
- Sugar 0.6 g
- Protein 154.7 g
- Cholesterol 250 mg

Parmesan Fish Fillets

Preparation Time: 10 minutes
Cooking Time: 15 minutes
Serve: 4

Ingredients:

- 4 cod fillets
- 2 tsp paprika
- 3/4 cup parmesan cheese, grated
- 1 tbsp olive oil
- 1 tbsp parsley, chopped
- 1/4 tsp sea salt

Directions:

1. In a shallow dish, mix together parmesan cheese, paprika, parsley, and salt.
2. Brush fish fillets with oil and coat with cheese mixture.
3. Place fish fillets on mesh rack then insert rack into the air fryer oven.
4. Set the temperature to 400 F and timer for 15 minutes. Press start.
5. Serve and enjoy.

Nutritional Value (Amount per Serving):

- Calories 265
- Fat 14.1 g
- Carbohydrates 2.2 g
- Sugar 0.1 g
- Protein 34.3 g
- Cholesterol 86 mg

Chipotle Shrimp

Preparation Time: 10 minutes
Cooking Time: 8 minutes
Serve: 4

Ingredients:

- 1 1/2 lbs shrimp, peeled and deveined
- 1 /4 tsp ground cumin
- 2 tsp chipotle in adobo
- 2 tbsp olive oil
- 4 tbsp lime juice

Directions:

1. Add shrimp, oil, lime juice, cumin, and chipotle in a zip-lock bag. Seal bag shake well and place it in the refrigerator for 30 minutes.
2. Thread marinated shrimp onto skewers and place on mesh rack then insert rack into the air fryer oven.
3. Select air fry mode then set the temperature to 350 F and timer for 8 minutes. Press start.
4. Serve and enjoy.

Nutritional Value (Amount per Serving):

- Calories 275
- Fat 10 g
- Carbohydrates 6.4 g
- Sugar 0.7 g
- Protein 39 g
- Cholesterol 359 mg

Horseradish Fish Fillets

Preparation Time: 10 minutes
Cooking Time: 7 minutes
Serve: 2

Ingredients:

- 2 salmon fillets
- 1/4 cup breadcrumbs
- 2 tbsp olive oil
- 1 tbsp horseradish
- Pepper
- Salt

Directions:

1. Place salmon fillets on a mesh rack.
2. In a small bowl, mix together breadcrumbs, oil, horseradish, pepper, and salt and spread over salmon fillets.
3. Insert the rack into the air fryer oven.
4. Select air fry mode then set the temperature to 400 F and timer for 7 minutes. Press start.
5. Serve and enjoy.

Nutritional Value (Amount per Serving):

- Calories 415
- Fat 25.8 g
- Carbohydrates 10.6 g
- Sugar 1.4 g
- Protein 36.4 g
- Cholesterol 78 mg

Cajun Shrimp

Preparation Time: 10 minutes
Cooking Time: 6 minutes
Serve: 2

Ingredients:

- 1/2 lb shrimp, peeled and deveined
- 1/2 tsp old bay seasoning
- 1/2 tsp cayenne pepper
- 1 tbsp olive oil
- 1/4 tsp paprika
- Pinch of salt

Directions:

1. Add shrimp and remaining ingredients into the mixing bowl and toss well to coat.
2. Add shrimp on mesh rack then insert rack into the air fryer oven.
3. Select air fry mode then set the temperature to 390 F and timer for 6 minutes. Press start.
4. Serve and enjoy.

Nutritional Value (Amount per Serving):

- Calories 197
- Fat 9 g
- Carbohydrates 2.1 g
- Sugar 0.1 g
- Protein 25.9 g
- Cholesterol 239 mg

Lemon Garlic Fish

Preparation Time: 10 minutes
Cooking Time: 10 minutes
Serve: 2

Ingredients:

- 12 oz white fish fillets
- 1/2 tsp garlic powder
- 1/2 tsp onion powder
- 1/2 tsp lemon pepper seasoning
- Pepper
- Salt

Directions:

1. Spray fish fillets with cooking spray and season with onion powder, lemon pepper seasoning, garlic powder, pepper, and salt.
2. Place fish on mesh rack then insert rack into the air fryer oven.
3. Select air fry mode then set the temperature to 360 F and timer for 6-10 minutes. Press start.
4. Serve and enjoy.

Nutritional Value (Amount per Serving):

- Calories 295
- Fat 12.8 g
- Carbohydrates 1.4 g
- Sugar 0.4 g
- Protein 41.9 g
- Cholesterol 131 mg

Bagel Fish Fillets

Preparation Time: 10 minutes
Cooking Time: 10 minutes
Serve: 4

Ingredients:

- 4 white fish fillets
- 2 tbsp almond flour
- 1/4 cup bagel seasoning
- 1 tbsp mayonnaise
- 1 tsp lemon pepper seasoning

Directions:

1. In a small bowl, mix together bagel seasoning, almond flour, and lemon pepper seasoning.
2. Brush mayonnaise over fish fillets. Sprinkle seasoning mixture over fish fillets.
3. Place fish fillets on mesh rack then insert rack into the air fryer oven.
4. Set the temperature to 400 F and timer for 10 minutes. Press start.
5. Serve and enjoy.

Nutritional Value (Amount per Serving):

- Calories 375
- Fat 2.5 g
- Carbohydrates 7.2 g
- Sugar 1 g
- Protein 41.3 g
- Cholesterol 120 mg

Chapter 5: Vegetables & Side Dishes

Easy Zucchini Patties

Preparation Time: 10 minutes
Cooking Time: 25 minutes
Serve: 6

Ingredients:

- 1 egg, lightly beaten
- 1/4 cup parmesan cheese, grated
- 1/2 tbsp Dijon mustard
- 1/2 tbsp mayonnaise
- 1 cup zucchini, shredded
- 2 tbsp onion, minced
- 1/2 cup breadcrumbs
- Pepper
- Salt

Directions:

1. Add all ingredients into the bowl and mix until well combined.
2. Make patties from the mixture and place on mesh rack then insert rack into the air fryer oven.
3. Set the temperature to 400 F and timer for 25 minutes. Press start.
4. Serve and enjoy.

Nutritional Value (Amount per Serving):

- Calories 80
- Fat 3.2 g
- Carbohydrates 7.9 g
- Sugar 1.2 g
- Protein 4.5 g
- Cholesterol 33 mg

Creamy Cauliflower

Preparation Time: 10 minutes
Cooking Time: 20 minutes
Serve: 4

Ingredients:

- 1 cauliflower head, cut into florets
- 1/2 cup mayonnaise
- 2 tsp Dijon mustard
- 1/4 cup sour cream
- 2 tbsp fresh lemon juice
- 1/2 cup cheddar cheese, shredded

Directions:

1. Spread cauliflower florets on a roasting pan and bake for 10 minutes.
2. In a mixing bowl, stir together cauliflower, lemon juice, cheese, mayonnaise, mustard, and sour cream and pour into the baking dish.
3. Place baking dish on mesh rack then insert rack into the air fryer oven.
4. Set the temperature to 375 F and timer for 20 minutes. Press start.
5. Serve and enjoy.

Nutritional Value (Amount per Serving):

- Calories 220
- Fat 17.7 g
- Carbohydrates 11.6 g
- Sugar 3.7 g
- Protein 5.7 g
- Cholesterol 29 mg

Sweet Potatoes & Apple

Preparation Time: 10 minutes
Cooking Time: 30 minutes
Serve: 2

Ingredients:

- 2 large green apples, diced
- 1 tbsp olive oil
- 2 tsp cinnamon
- 2 large sweet potatoes, diced
- 2 tbsp maple syrup

Directions:

1. In a mixing bowl, toss sweet potatoes, apples, cinnamon, and oil.
2. Spread sweet potatoes and apples on mesh rack then insert rack into the air fryer oven.
3. Set the temperature to 400 F and timer for 30 minutes. Press start.
4. Drizzle with maple syrup and serve.

Nutritional Value (Amount per Serving):

- Calories 351
- Fat 7 g
- Carbohydrates 75 g
- Sugar 35 g
- Protein 2 g
- Cholesterol 0 mg

Broccoli Fritters

Preparation Time: 10 minutes
Cooking Time: 30 minutes
Serve: 4

Ingredients:

- 3 cups broccoli florets, cooked & chopped
- ¼ cup breadcrumbs
- 2 cups cheddar cheese, shredded
- 2 garlic cloves, minced
- 2 eggs, lightly beaten
- Pepper
- Salt

Directions:

1. Add all ingredients into the large bowl and mix until well combined.
2. Make patties from mixture and place on mesh rack then insert rack into the air fryer oven.
3. Set the temperature to 375 F and timer for 30 minutes. Press start.
4. Serve and enjoy.

Nutritional Value (Amount per Serving):

- Calories 295
- Fat 20 g
- Carbohydrates 6 g
- Sugar 1.7 g
- Protein 19.2 g
- Cholesterol 141 mg

Baked Brussel Sprouts

Preparation Time: 10 minutes
Cooking Time: 40 minutes
Serve: 6

Ingredients:

- 1 ½ lb Brussels sprouts, cut ends & sliced in half
- 2 tbsp olive oil
- 1 lemon juice
- 1 tsp garlic powder
- Pepper
- Salt

Directions:

1. In a bowl, toss Brussels sprouts with garlic powder, oil, pepper, and salt.
2. Add Brussels sprouts into the baking dish.
3. Place baking dish on mesh rack then insert rack into the air fryer oven.
4. Set the temperature to 400 F and timer for 35-40 minutes. Press start.
5. Drizzle lemon juice over Brussels sprouts and serve.

Nutritional Value (Amount per Serving):

- Calories 91
- Fat 5.1 g
- Carbohydrates 10.7 g
- Sugar 2.6 g
- Protein 4 g
- Cholesterol 0 mg

Curried Cauliflower Florets

Preparation Time: 10 minutes
Cooking Time: 15 minutes
Serve: 4

Ingredients:

- 2 lbs cauliflower, cut into florets
- 1 1/2 tsp curry powder
- 2 tsp fresh lemon juice
- 1 tbsp olive oil
- 1 tsp kosher salt

Directions:

1. Toss cauliflower florets with curry powder, oil, and salt.
2. Spread cauliflower florets on mesh rack then insert rack into the air fryer oven.
3. Set the temperature to 400 F and timer for 15 minutes. Press start.
4. Drizzle with lemon juice and serve.

Nutritional Value (Amount per Serving):

- Calories 90
- Fat 4 g
- Carbohydrates 12 g
- Sugar 5 g
- Protein 4 g
- Cholesterol 0 mg

Zucchini Bake

Preparation Time: 10 minutes
Cooking Time: 45 minutes
Serve: 6

Ingredients:

- 3 zucchini, grated
- 1/2 cup mozzarella cheese, shredded
- 1/2 cup feta cheese, crumbled
- 1/2 cup dill, chopped
- 3 tbsp butter, melted
- 1/2 cup flour
- 3 eggs, lightly beaten
- Pepper
- Salt

Directions:

1. In a mixing bowl, mix together zucchini, cheeses, dill, eggs, butter, pepper, flour, and salt.
2. Pour the zucchini mixture into the baking dish.
3. Place baking dish on mesh rack then insert rack into the air fryer oven.
4. Set the temperature to 350 F and timer for 45 minutes. Press start.
5. Serve and enjoy.

Nutritional Value (Amount per Serving):

- Calories 186
- Fat 11.5 g
- Carbohydrates 14.2 g
- Sugar 2.4 g
- Protein 8.4 g
- Cholesterol 109 mg

Easy Baked Potatoes

Preparation Time: 10 minutes
Cooking Time: 40 minutes
Serve: 4

Ingredients:

- 4 potatoes, scrubbed and washed
- ½ tbsp butter, melted
- ¾ tsp garlic powder
- ½ tsp Italian seasoning
- ½ tsp sea salt

Directions:

1. Prick potatoes using a fork.
2. Rub potatoes with melted butter and sprinkle with garlic powder, Italian seasoning, and sea salt.
3. Arrange potatoes on mesh rack then insert rack into the air fryer oven.
4. Set the temperature to 400 F and timer for 40 minutes. Press start.
5. Serve and enjoy.

Nutritional Value (Amount per Serving):

- Calories 163
- Fat 1.8 g
- Carbohydrates 33.9 g
- Sugar 2.6 g
- Protein 3.7 g
- Cholesterol 4 mg

Healthy Butternut Squash

Preparation Time: 10 minutes
Cooking Time: 40 minutes
Serve: 4

Ingredients:

- 3 lbs butternut squash, peeled, seeded, and cut into 1-inch cubes
- 1 1/2 tbsp olive oil
- 1/2 tsp cinnamon
- 1 1/2 tbsp maple syrup
- Pepper
- Salt

Directions:

1. In a mixing bowl, toss squash cubes with the remaining ingredients.
2. Spread squash cubes mesh rack then insert rack into the air fryer oven.
3. Set the temperature to 400 F and timer for 35-40 minutes. Press start.
4. Serve and enjoy.

Nutritional Value (Amount per Serving):

- Calories 219
- Fat 5.6 g
- Carbohydrates 45.1 g
- Sugar 12 g
- Protein 3.4 g
- Cholesterol 0 mg

Baked Carrots

Preparation Time: 10 minutes
Cooking Time: 30 minutes
Serve: 4

Ingredients:

- 24 baby carrots
- 1 tsp cinnamon
- 6 tbsp butter, melted
- 1/4 cup brown sugar
- Pepper
- Salt

Directions:

1. Arrange baby carrots in the baking dish. Pour melted butter over baby carrots.
2. Sprinkle cinnamon, brown sugar, pepper, and salt over baby carrots.
3. Place baking dish on mesh rack then insert rack into the air fryer oven.
4. Set the temperature to 390 F and timer for 25-30 minutes. Press start.
5. Serve and enjoy.

Nutritional Value (Amount per Serving):

- Calories 210
- Fat 17.4 g
- Carbohydrates 14.3 g
- Sugar 11.7 g
- Protein 0.6 g
- Cholesterol 46 mg

Chapter 6: Snacks & Appetizers

Spicy Lime Chickpeas

Preparation Time: 10 minutes
Cooking Time: 12 minutes
Serve: 4

Ingredients:

- 14 oz can chickpeas, rinsed, drained and pat dry
- 1/2 tsp chili powder
- 1 tbsp olive oil
- 1 tbsp lime juice
- 1/4 tsp red pepper
- Pepper
- Salt

Directions:

1. Add chickpeas, red pepper, chili powder, oil, pepper, and salt into the mixing bowl and toss well.
2. Place chickpeas on mesh rack then insert rack into the air fryer oven.
3. Select air fryer mode then set the temperature to 375 F and timer for 12 minutes. Press start. Stir halfway through.
4. Drizzle lemon juice over chickpeas and serve.

Nutritional Value (Amount per Serving):

- Calories 154
- Fat 4.7 g
- Carbohydrates 24.1 g
- Sugar 0.6 g
- Protein 5.1 g
- Cholesterol 0 mg

Healthy Cashew Nuts

Preparation Time: 10 minutes
Cooking Time: 5 minutes
Serve: 6

Ingredients:

- 3 cups cashews
- 1 tsp ground coriander
- 1 tsp paprika
- 2 tbsp olive oil
- 1 tsp ground cumin
- 1 tsp salt

Directions:

1. Add cashews and remaining ingredients into the mixing bowl and toss well.
2. Spread cashews on mesh rack then insert rack into the air fryer oven.
3. Select air fryer mode then set the temperature to 330 F and timer for 5 minutes. Press start. Stir halfway through.
4. Serve and enjoy.

Nutritional Value (Amount per Serving):

- Calories 436
- Fat 36.6 g
- Carbohydrates 22.7 g
- Sugar 3.5 g
- Protein 10.6 g
- Cholesterol 0 mg

Corn Dip

Preparation Time: 10 minutes
Cooking Time: 20 minutes
Serve: 6

Ingredients:

- 15 oz can corn kernel, drained
- ½ cup cheddar cheese, shredded
- 1 tsp smoked paprika
- ¼ cup sour cream
- 1 tbsp green chilies, diced
- 2 green onions, sliced
- ½ bell pepper, diced
- 1/3 cup mayonnaise

Directions:

1. Add all ingredients into the mixing bowl and mix until well combined.
2. Pour mixture into the baking dish.
3. Place a baking dish on a mesh rack then insert the rack into the air fryer oven.
4. Set the temperature to 350 F and timer for 20 minutes. Press start.
5. Serve with enjoy.

Nutritional Value (Amount per Serving):

- Calories 175
- Fat 10.3 g
- Carbohydrates 18.6 g
- Sugar 3.9 g
- Protein 4.9 g
- Cholesterol 18 mg

Spicy Peanuts

Preparation Time: 10 minutes
Cooking Time: 10 minutes
Serve: 4

Ingredients:

- 1 cup peanuts
- ¼ tsp chili powder
- 2 tbsp olive oil
- Salt

Directions:

1. In a bowl, toss peanuts, oil, chili powder, and salt.
2. Place peanuts on mesh rack then insert rack into the air fryer oven.
3. Select air fryer mode then set the temperature to 320 F and timer for 10 minutes. Press start. Stir halfway through.
4. Serve and enjoy.

Nutritional Value (Amount per Serving):

- Calories 267
- Fat 25 g
- Carbohydrates 5.9 g
- Sugar 1.5 g
- Protein 9.4 g
- Cholesterol 0 mg

Vegetable Fritters

Preparation Time: 10 minutes
Cooking Time: 15 minutes
Serve: 2

Ingredients:

- 1 egg, lightly beaten
- 1 1/2 cups frozen vegetable, cooked & mashed
- 1/2 tbsp coconut flour
- 1/4 tsp garlic powder
- 1/4 cup parmesan cheese, shredded
- Pepper
- Salt

Directions:

1. Add mash vegetables and egg in a bowl and mix well.
2. Add parmesan cheese, coconut flour, garlic powder, pepper, and salt and stir well.
3. Make patties from the mixture and place on mesh rack then insert rack into the air fryer oven.
4. Select air fryer mode then set the temperature to 390 F and timer for 15 minutes. Press start.
5. Serve and enjoy.

Nutritional Value (Amount per Serving):

- Calories 183
- Fat 6.2 g
- Carbohydrates 20.7 g
- Sugar 4.8 g
- Protein 11 g
- Cholesterol 89 mg

Ricotta Cheese Dip

Preparation Time: 10 minutes
Cooking Time: 20 minutes
Serve: 6

Ingredients:

- 2 cups ricotta cheese
- 2 tsp fresh thyme, chopped
- 1 lemon zest
- ¼ cup parmesan cheese, shredded
- ½ cup mozzarella cheese, shredded
- 3 tbsp olive oil
- 2 garlic cloves, minced
- Pepper
- Salt

Directions:

1. Add all ingredients into the bowl and mix until well combined.
2. Pour mixture into the baking dish.
3. Place a baking dish on a mesh rack then insert the rack into the air fryer oven.
4. Set the temperature to 375 F and timer for 20 minutes. Press start.
5. Serve and enjoy.

Nutritional Value (Amount per Serving):

- Calories 183
- Fat 14 g
- Carbohydrates 4.9 g
- Sugar 0.3 g
- Protein 10.2 g
- Cholesterol 27 mg

Tasty Ranch Chickpeas

Preparation Time: 10 minutes
Cooking Time: 12 minutes
Serve: 4

Ingredients:

- 14.5 oz can chickpeas, rinsed, drained and pat dry
- 1 1/2 tsp ranch seasoning
- Pepper
- Salt

Directions:

1. Add chickpeas, ranch seasoning, pepper, and salt into the mixing bowl and toss well.
2. Spread chickpeas on mesh rack then insert rack into the air fryer oven.
3. Select air fryer mode then set the temperature to 375 F and timer for 12 minutes. Press start. Stir halfway through.
4. Serve and enjoy.

Nutritional Value (Amount per Serving):

- Calories 120
- Fat 1.1 g
- Carbohydrates 22.5 g
- Sugar 0 g
- Protein 4.9 g
- Cholesterol 0 mg

Carrot Fries

Preparation Time: 10 minutes
Cooking Time: 15 minutes
Serve: 4

Ingredients:

- 4 carrots, peeled and cut into fries
- 2 tbsp olive oil
- 2 tbsp parmesan cheese, grated
- 1 1/2 tbsp garlic, minced
- Pepper
- Salt

Directions:

1. Add carrots and remaining ingredients into the mixing bowl and toss well.
2. Place carrot fries on mesh rack then insert rack into the air fryer oven.
3. Select air fryer mode then set the temperature to 350 F and timer for 15 minutes. Press start. Stir halfway through.
4. Serve and enjoy.

Nutritional Value (Amount per Serving):

- Calories 99
- Fat 7.6 g
- Carbohydrates 7.2 g
- Sugar 3 g
- Protein 1.6 g
- Cholesterol 2 mg

Flavorful Potato Wedges

Preparation Time: 10 minutes
Cooking Time: 24 minutes
Serve: 2

Ingredients:

- 1/2 lb potatoes, cut into wedges
- ¼ tsp chili powder
- 1 tbsp olive oil
- Pepper
- Salt

Directions:

1. In a bowl, toss potato wedges with oil, chili powder, pepper, and salt.
2. Place Potato wedges on mesh rack then insert rack into the air fryer oven.
3. Select air fryer mode then set the temperature to 390 F and timer for 24 minutes. Press start. Stir halfway through.
4. Serve and enjoy.

Nutritional Value (Amount per Serving):

- Calories 138
- Fat 7.1 g
- Carbohydrates 17.9 g
- Sugar 1.3 g
- Protein 1.9 g
- Cholesterol 0 mg

Mexican Cheese Dip

Preparation Time: 10 minutes
Cooking Time: 30 minutes
Serve: 10

Ingredients:

- 16 oz cream cheese, softened
- 3 cups cheddar cheese, shredded
- 1 cup sour cream
- 1/2 cup salsa

Directions:

1. In a mixing bowl, mix together all ingredients until well combined and pour into the baking dish.
2. Place a baking dish on a mesh rack then insert the rack into the air fryer oven.
3. Set the temperature to 350 F and timer for 30 minutes. Press start.
4. Serve and enjoy.

Nutritional Value (Amount per Serving):

- Calories 348
- Fat 31.9 g
- Carbohydrates 3.4 g
- Sugar 0.7 g
- Protein 12.8 g
- Cholesterol 96 mg

Spicy Cheese Dip

Preparation Time: 10 minutes
Cooking Time: 20 minutes
Serve: 14

Ingredients:

- 8.5 oz can green chilies
- ¼ tsp cumin
- 1 tsp garlic, minced
- 15 oz cream cheese, softened
- ¼ tsp pepper
- 2 cups cheddar cheese, shredded
- ¼ tsp salt

Directions:

1. Add all ingredients into the mixing bowl and mix until well combined.
2. Pour mixture into the baking dish.
3. Place a baking dish on a mesh rack then insert the rack into the air fryer oven.
4. Set the temperature to 350 F and timer for 20 minutes. Press start.
5. Serve and enjoy.

Nutritional Value (Amount per Serving):

- Calories 175
- Fat 16 g
- Carbohydrates 2 g
- Sugar 1 g
- Protein 6 g
- Cholesterol 53 mg

Maple Chickpeas

Preparation Time: 10 minutes
Cooking Time: 12 minutes
Serve: 4

Ingredients:

- 14 oz can chickpeas, rinsed, drained and pat dry
- 1 tbsp maple syrup
- 1 tbsp olive oil
- 1 tsp ground cinnamon
- 1 tbsp brown sugar
- Pepper
- Salt

Directions:

1. Spread chickpeas on mesh rack then insert rack into the air fryer oven.
2. Select air fryer mode then set the temperature to 375 F and timer for 12 minutes. Press start. Stir halfway through.
3. In a mixing bowl, mix together cinnamon, brown sugar, maple syrup, oil, pepper, and salt. Add chickpeas and toss well to coat.
4. Serve and enjoy.

Nutritional Value (Amount per Serving):

- Calories 171
- Fat 4.7 g
- Carbohydrates 28.5 g
- Sugar 5.2 g
- Protein 4.9 g
- Cholesterol 0 mg

Simple French Fries

Preparation Time: 10 minutes
Cooking Time: 15 minutes
Serve: 4

Ingredients:

- 2 potatoes, peel & cut into fries shape
- 1/2 tbsp olive oil
- 1/2 tsp garlic powder
- Pepper
- Salt

Directions:

1. Soak potato fries in water for 15 minutes. Drain well and pat dry with a paper towel.
2. Toss potato fries with oil, garlic powder, pepper, and salt.
3. Spread potato fries on mesh rack then insert rack into the air fryer oven.
4. Select air fryer mode then set the temperature to 375 F and timer for 15 minutes. Press start. Stir halfway through.
5. Serve and enjoy.

Nutritional Value (Amount per Serving):

- Calories 90
- Fat 1.9 g
- Carbohydrates 17 g
- Sugar 1.3 g
- Protein 1.9 g
- Cholesterol 0 mg

Zucchini Bites

Preparation Time: 10 minutes
Cooking Time: 10 minutes
Serve: 4

Ingredients:

- 1 cup breadcrumbs
- 1 egg, lightly beaten
- 4 zucchini, grated
- 1 tsp Italian seasoning
- 1/2 cup parmesan cheese, grated

Directions:

1. Add all ingredients into the bowl and mix until well combined.
2. Make small balls from the zucchini mixture and place on mesh rack then insert rack into the air fryer oven.
3. Select air fryer mode then set the temperature to 400 F and timer for 10 minutes. Press start.
4. Serve and enjoy.

Nutritional Value (Amount per Serving):

- Calories 193
- Fat 5.6 g
- Carbohydrates 26.6 g
- Sugar 5.2 g
- Protein 11 g
- Cholesterol 50 mg

Broccoli Pop-corn

Preparation Time: 10 minutes
Cooking Time: 6 minutes
Serve: 4

Ingredients:

- 4 eggs yolks
- 2 cups broccoli florets
- 2 cups coconut flour
- Pepper
- Salt

Directions:

1. In a small bowl, whisk eggs with pepper and salt.
2. In a shallow dish, add coconut flour.
3. Dip broccoli floret with egg and coat with coconut flour and place on mesh rack then insert rack into the air fryer oven.
4. Select air fryer mode then set the temperature to 400 F and timer for 6 minutes. Press start.
5. Serve and enjoy.

Nutritional Value (Amount per Serving):

- Calories 310
- Fat 10.8 g
- Carbohydrates 43.3 g
- Sugar 0.9 g
- Protein 12.1 g
- Cholesterol 194 mg

Chapter 7: Dehydrated

Broccoli Florets

Preparation Time: 10 minutes
Cooking Time: 12 hours
Serve: 6

Ingredients:

- 1 lb broccoli florets

Directions:

1. Arrange broccoli florets on mesh racks then place racks in air fryer oven.
2. Select dehydrate mode then set the temperature to 115 F and time for 12 hours.
3. Store in air-tight container.

Nutritional Value (Amount per Serving):

- Calories 25
- Fat 0.3 g
- Carbohydrates 5 g
- Sugar 1.3 g
- Protein 2.1 g
- Cholesterol 0 mg

Kiwi Slices

Preparation Time: 5 minutes
Cooking Time: 10 hours
Serve: 4

Ingredients:

- 5 kiwis, peeled & cut into 1/4-inch thick slices

Directions:

1. Arrange kiwi slices on mesh racks then place racks in air fryer oven.
2. Select dehydrate mode then set the temperature to 135 F and time for 10 hours.
3. Store in air-tight container.

Nutritional Value (Amount per Serving):

- Calories 71
- Fat 0.6 g
- Carbohydrates 16 g
- Sugar 10.3 g
- Protein 1.3 g
- Cholesterol 0 mg

Dragon Fruit Slices

Preparation Time: 10 minutes
Cooking Time: 12 hours
Serve: 4

Ingredients:

- 2 dragon fruit, peel & cut into 1/4-inch thick slices

Directions:

1. Arrange dragon fruit slices on mesh racks then place racks in air fryer oven.
2. Select dehydrate mode then set the temperature to 115 F and time for 12 hours.
3. Store in air-tight container.

Nutritional Value (Amount per Serving):

- Calories 25
- Fat 0 g
- Carbohydrates 6 g
- Sugar 6 g
- Protein 0 g
- Cholesterol 0 mg

Sweet Potato Chips

Preparation Time: 10 minutes
Cooking Time: 12 hours
Serve: 2

Ingredients:

- 2 sweet potatoes, peel and sliced thinly
- 1/8 tsp cinnamon
- 1 tsp olive oil
- Salt

Directions:

1. Add sweet potato slices in a bowl. Add cinnamon, oil, and salt and toss well.
2. Arrange sweet potato slices on mesh racks then place racks in air fryer oven.
3. Select dehydrate mode then set the temperature to 125 F and time for 12 hours.
4. Store in air-tight container.

Nutritional Value (Amount per Serving):

- Calories 195
- Fat 2 g
- Carbohydrates 41 g
- Sugar 0.8 g
- Protein 2.3 g
- Cholesterol 0 mg

Candied Pecans

Preparation Time: 10 minutes
Cooking Time: 12 hours
Serve: 4

Ingredients:

- 1 cup pecan halves, soaked in water overnight
- Pinch of cinnamon
- 6 tbsp maple syrup

Directions:

1. In a bowl, toss pecan with maple syrup and cinnamon.
2. Arrange pecans on mesh racks then place racks in air fryer oven.
3. Select dehydrate mode then set the temperature to 105 F and time for 12 hours.
4. Store in air-tight container.

Nutritional Value (Amount per Serving):

- Calories 103
- Fat 2.6 g
- Carbohydrates 20.7 g
- Sugar 18 g
- Protein 0.4 g
- Cholesterol 0 mg

Green Beans

Preparation Time: 10 minutes
Cooking Time: 8 hours
Serve: 4

Ingredients:

- 2 1/2 lbs green beans, frozen & thawed

Directions:

1. Arrange green beans on mesh racks then place racks in air fryer oven.
2. Select dehydrate mode then set the temperature to 135 F and time for 8 hours.
3. Store in air-tight container.

Nutritional Value (Amount per Serving):

- Calories 104
- Fat 8.5 g
- Carbohydrates 6.3 g
- Sugar 3.1 g
- Protein 1.5 g
- Cholesterol 0 mg

Mango Slices

Preparation Time: 10 minutes
Cooking Time: 12 hours
Serve: 4

Ingredients:

- 2 mangoes, peel & cut into slices

Directions:

1. Arrange mango slices on mesh racks then place racks in air fryer oven.
2. Select dehydrate mode then set the temperature to 135 F and time for 12 hours.
3. Store in air-tight container.

Nutritional Value (Amount per Serving):

- Calories 101
- Fat 0.6 g
- Carbohydrates 25.2 g
- Sugar 23 g
- Protein 1.4 g
- Cholesterol 0 mg

Eggplant Slices

Preparation Time: 10 minutes
Cooking Time: 4 hours
Serve: 4

Ingredients:

- 1 eggplant, cut into 1/4-inch thick slices

Directions:

1. Arrange eggplant slices on mesh racks then place racks in air fryer oven.
2. Select dehydrate mode then set the temperature to 145 F and time for 4 hours.
3. Store in air-tight container.

Nutritional Value (Amount per Serving):

- Calories 29
- Fat 0.2 g
- Carbohydrates 6.7 g
- Sugar 3.4 g
- Protein 1.1 g
- Cholesterol 0 mg

Apple Slices

Preparation Time: 10 minutes
Cooking Time: 8 hours
Serve: 5

Ingredients:

- 4 green apples, cored & cut into 8-inch thick slices
- 1/2 tsp ground cinnamon

Directions:

1. Arrange apple slices on mesh racks and sprinkle with cinnamon then place racks in air fryer oven.
2. Select dehydrate mode then set the temperature to 145 F and time for 8 hours.
3. Store in air-tight container.

Nutritional Value (Amount per Serving):

- Calories 95
- Fat 0.3 g
- Carbohydrates 25 g
- Sugar 18.6 g
- Protein 0.5 g
- Cholesterol 0 mg

Beet Chips

Preparation Time: 10 minutes
Cooking Time: 8 hours
Serve: 4

Ingredients:

- 4 medium beets, peel & cut into slices
- 1 tbsp salt

Directions:

1. Arrange beet slices on mesh racks and sprinkle with salt then place racks in air fryer oven.
2. Select dehydrate mode then set the temperature to 135 F and time for 8 hours.
3. Store in air-tight container.

Nutritional Value (Amount per Serving):

- Calories 44
- Fat 0.2 g
- Carbohydrates 10 g
- Sugar 8 g
- Protein 1.7 g
- Cholesterol 0 mg

Chapter 8: Desserts

Lemon Brownies

Preparation Time: 10 minutes
Cooking Time: 20 minutes
Serve: 16

Ingredients:

- 2 eggs
- ¾ cup all-purpose flour
- 1 tbsp fresh lemon juice
- ½ tsp baking powder
- ½ lemon zest
- ¾ cup sugar
- ½ cup butter, softened

Directions:

1. In a large bowl, beat sugar, butter, and lemon zest until fluffy.
2. Add eggs, lemon juice, and flour and mix until combined.
3. Pour batter into the greased baking pan and spread evenly.
4. Place the pan on a mesh rack then insert the rack into the air fryer oven.
5. Set the temperature to 350 F and timer for 20 minutes. Press start.
6. Serve and enjoy.

Nutritional Value (Amount per Serving):

- Calories 116
- Fat 6.4 g
- Carbohydrates 14 g
- Sugar 9.5 g
- Protein 1.4 g
- Cholesterol 36 mg

Chocolate Cake

Preparation Time: 10 minutes
Cooking Time: 25 minutes
Serve: 8

Ingredients:

- 1 egg
- 3 tbsp cocoa powder
- 1 cup of sugar
- 1 cup all-purpose flour
- 1 tsp baking soda
- 1 tsp baking powder
- 1 tsp vanilla
- 1/4 cup butter
- 1 cup boiling water
- 1/4 tsp salt

Directions:

1. Spray a baking dish with cooking spray and set aside.
2. Add butter and boiling water in a bowl and beat until butter is melted.
3. Add vanilla and egg and beat until well combined.
4. In a medium bowl, mix together flour, baking soda, baking powder, cocoa powder, sugar, and salt.
5. Add egg mixture into the flour mixture and beat until well combined.
6. Pour batter into prepared baking dish.
7. Place a baking dish on a mesh rack then insert the rack into the air fryer oven.
8. Set the temperature to 350 F and timer for 25 minutes. Press start.
9. Serve and enjoy.

Nutritional Value (Amount per Serving):

- Calories 216
- Fat 6.7 g
- Carbohydrates 38.5 g
- Sugar 25.2 g
- Protein 2.7 g
- Cholesterol 36 mg

Baked Spiced Apples

Preparation Time: 10 minutes
Cooking Time: 10 minutes
Serve: 4

Ingredients:

- 4 apples, sliced
- 2 tbsp butter, melted
- 1 tsp apple pie spice
- 2 tbsp sugar

Directions:

1. Add apple slices into the mixing bowl. Add remaining ingredients on top of apple slices and toss until well coated.
2. Place apple slices in a baking pan.
3. Place baking pan on mesh rack then insert rack into the air fryer oven.
4. Set the temperature to 350 F and timer for 10 minutes. Press start.
5. Serve and enjoy.

Nutritional Value (Amount per Serving):

- Calories 196
- Fat 6.8 g
- Carbohydrates 37.1 g
- Sugar 29.2 g
- Protein 0.6 g
- Cholesterol 16 mg

Brownie Muffins

Preparation Time: 10 minutes
Cooking Time: 15 minutes
Serve: 6

Ingredients:

- 3 eggs
- 1/2 cup Swerve
- 1 cup almond flour
- 1 tbsp gelatin
- 1/3 cup butter, melted
- 1/3 cup cocoa powder

Directions:

1. Line the muffin pan with cupcake liners and set aside.
2. Add all ingredients into the bowl and stir until just combined.
3. Pour batter into the prepared muffin pan.
4. Place muffin pan on mesh rack then insert rack into the air fryer oven.
5. Set the temperature to 350 F and timer for 15 minutes. Press start.
6. Serve and enjoy.

Nutritional Value (Amount per Serving):

- Calories 165
- Fat 15 g
- Carbohydrates 4 g
- Sugar 0.5 g
- Protein 6 g
- Cholesterol 110 mg

Delicious Brownies

Preparation Time: 10 minutes
Cooking Time: 30 minutes
Serve: 6

Ingredients:

- 2 eggs
- 1 cup brown sugar
- 2 tsp vanilla
- 1/4 cup cocoa powder
- 1/2 cup butter, melted
- 1/2 cup walnuts, chopped
- 1/4 cup all-purpose flour
- 1/8 tsp salt

Directions:

1. Spray a baking dish with cooking spray and set aside.
2. In a bowl, whisk eggs with vanilla, butter, and cocoa powder.
3. Add flour, walnuts, sugar, and salt and stir until well combined.
4. Pour batter into the prepared baking dish.
5. Place a baking dish on a mesh rack then insert the rack into the air fryer oven.
6. Set the temperature to 320 F and timer for 30 minutes. Press start.
7. Serve and enjoy.

Nutritional Value (Amount per Serving):

- Calories 344
- Fat 23.5 g
- Carbohydrates 31 g
- Sugar 23.9 g
- Protein 5.7 g
- Cholesterol 95 mg

Moist Peanut Butter Muffins

Preparation Time: 10 minutes
Cooking Time: 20 minutes
Serve: 12

Ingredients:

- 1 egg
- 1 1/2 tsp vanilla
- 2 1/2 tsp baking powder
- 2/3 cup brown sugar
- 1 3/4 cups flour
- 1/4 cup oil
- 2/3 cup peanut butter
- 3/4 cup milk
- 1/4 tsp salt

Directions:

1. In a bowl, mix together flour, baking powder, brown sugar, and salt.
2. In a small bowl, whisk egg, vanilla, oil, peanut butter, and milk.
3. Pour egg mixture into the flour mixture and mix until well combined.
4. Pour batter into the 12 silicone muffin molds.
5. Place muffin molds on mesh rack then insert rack into the air fryer oven.
6. Set the temperature to 350 F and timer for 20 minutes. Press start.
7. Serve and enjoy.

Nutritional Value (Amount per Serving):

- Calories 237
- Fat 12.6 g
- Carbohydrates 26 g
- Sugar 10 g
- Protein 6.4 g
- Cholesterol 15 mg

Simple Vanilla Muffins

Preparation Time: 10 minutes
Cooking Time: 20 minutes
Serve: 12

Ingredients:

- 3 eggs
- 1/2 cup butter
- 2/3 cup sugar
- 1 1/2 tsp baking powder
- 1/4 cup milk
- 1 tsp vanilla
- 1 1/2 cups all-purpose flour
- 1/4 tsp salt

Directions:

1. Line the muffin pan with cupcake liners and set aside.
2. In a bowl, mix flour, salt, and baking powder and set aside.
3. In a separate bowl, beat the sugar and butter until fluffy.
4. Add eggs one by one and beat until well combined.
5. Add flour mixture and beat until well combined.
6. Add milk, vanilla, and remaining flour mixture and beat until completely incorporated.
7. Pour mixture into the prepared muffin pan.
8. Place muffin pan on mesh rack then insert rack into the air fryer oven.
9. Set the temperature to 350 F and timer for 20 minutes. Press start.
10. Serve and enjoy.

Nutritional Value (Amount per Serving):

- Calories 186
- Fat 9 g
- Carbohydrates 23 g
- Sugar 11.5 g
- Protein 3.2 g
- Cholesterol 62 mg

Easy Baked Donuts

Preparation Time: 10 minutes
Cooking Time: 8 minutes
Serve: 6

Ingredients:

- 2 eggs
- 1/4 tsp cinnamon
- 1/4 tsp nutmeg
- 2 tsp baking powder
- 3/4 cup sugar
- 2 tbsp butter, melted
- 1 tsp vanilla
- 3/4 cup buttermilk
- 2 cups flour
- 1 tsp salt

Directions:

1. In a bowl, whisk eggs, butter, vanilla, and buttermilk until well combined.
2. In a large bowl, mix together flour, cinnamon, nutmeg, baking powder, sugar, and salt.
3. Pour egg mixture into the flour mixture and mix until well combined.
4. Pour batter into the 6 silicone donut molds.
5. Place donut molds on mesh rack then insert rack into the air fryer oven.
6. Set the temperature to 325 F and timer for 8 minutes. Press start.
7. Serve and enjoy.

Nutritional Value (Amount per Serving):

- Calories 317
- Fat 6 g
- Carbohydrates 59.4 g
- Sugar 26.8 g
- Protein 7.2 g
- Cholesterol 66 mg

Lemon Muffins

Preparation Time: 10 minutes
Cooking Time: 20 minutes
Serve: 12

Ingredients:

- 1 egg
- 1 tsp vanilla
- 1 cup Greek yogurt
- 1/3 cup butter, melted
- 1/3 cup fresh lemon juice
- 2 tbsp lemon zest
- ¾ tsp baking soda
- 1 tsp baking powder
- ½ cup sugar
- 1 ¾ cups all-purpose flour
- ¼ tsp salt

Directions:

1. Line 12-cup muffin pan with cupcake liners and set aside.
2. Add all dry ingredients into the mixing bowl and mix until well combined.
3. In a separate bowl, mix all wet ingredients. Add dry ingredient mixture into the wet ingredient mixture and mix until combined.
4. Spoon batter into the prepared muffin pan.
5. Place muffin pan on mesh rack then insert rack into the air fryer oven.
6. Set the temperature to 400 F and timer for 20 minutes. Press start.
7. Serve and enjoy.

Nutritional Value (Amount per Serving):

- Calories 160
- Fat 6.4 g
- Carbohydrates 23.2 g
- Sugar 8.9 g
- Protein 2.7 g
- Cholesterol 27 mg

Baked Blueberry Donuts

Preparation Time: 10 minutes
Cooking Time: 10 minutes
Serve: 6

Ingredients:

- 1 egg
- 3 tbsp yogurt
- 1/2 tsp vanilla
- 3 tbsp butter, melted
- 1/4 cup blueberries
- 1/4 cup milk
- 1/3 cup sugar
- 1/4 tsp baking soda
- 3/4 tsp baking powder
- 1 cup flour
- Pinch of salt

Directions:

1. In a bowl, mix together flour, sugar, baking soda, baking powder, and salt.
2. In a separate bowl, whisk an egg with butter, vanilla, yogurt, and milk until smooth.
3. Pour wet ingredients mixture into the flour mixture and mix until smooth.
4. Add blueberries and stir well.
5. Pour batter into the 6 silicone donut molds.
6. Place donut molds on mesh rack then insert rack into the air fryer oven.
7. Set the temperature to 350 F and timer for 10 minutes. Press start.
8. Serve and enjoy.

Nutritional Value (Amount per Serving):

- Calories 194
- Fat 7 g
- Carbohydrates 29.3 g
- Sugar 12.9 g
- Protein 4 g
- Cholesterol 44 mg

Chapter 9: 30-Day Meal Plan

Day 1

Breakfast- Herb Egg Muffins

Lunch-Parmesan Fish Fillets

Dinner-Beef Fajitas

Day 2

Breakfast- Breakfast Cheese Egg Bake

Lunch-Crispy Chicken Wings

Dinner-Lamb Cutlets

Day 3

Breakfast- Spicy Egg Bite

Lunch-Juicy Baked Cod

Dinner-Beef Fajitas

Day 4

Breakfast- Delicious Gruyere Cheese Bacon Egg Bite

Lunch- Delicious Mustard Chicken

Dinner-Garlic Lemon Lamb Chops

Day 5

Breakfast- Healthy Zucchini Frittata

Lunch-Bagel Fish Fillets

Dinner-Creole Chops

Day 6

Breakfast- Cheesy Breakfast Quiche

Lunch-Lemon Garlic Chicken

Dinner-BBQ Pork Chops

Day 7

Breakfast- Breakfast Cheese Egg Bake

Lunch-Tuna Steaks

Dinner-Easy Ranch Pork Chops

Day 8

Breakfast- Herb Egg Muffins

Lunch-Perfect Chicken Tenders

Dinner-Healthy & Juicy Pork Chops

Day 9

Breakfast- Baked Breakfast Donuts

Lunch-Chipotle Shrimp

Dinner-Herb Pork Chops

Day 10

Breakfast- Strawberry Donuts

Lunch-Herb Chicken Wings

Dinner- Tasty Pork Ribs

Day 11

Breakfast- Spicy Egg Bite

Lunch-Shrimp Fajitas

Dinner-Tasty Pork Ribs

Day 12

Breakfast- Delicious Gruyere Cheese Bacon Egg Bite

Lunch-Cajun Chicken

Dinner-Herb Pork Chops

Day 13

Breakfast- Baked Omelet

Lunch-Lemon Garlic Fish

Dinner-Spiced Pork Chops

Day 14

Breakfast- Healthy Zucchini Frittata

Lunch-Spicy Chicken Wings

Dinner-Tasty Pork Ribs

Day 15

Breakfast- Healthy Oatmeal Muffins

Lunch-Horseradish Fish Fillets

Dinner-Spiced Pork Chops

Day 16

Breakfast- Herb Egg Muffins

Lunch-Parmesan Fish Fillets

Dinner-Beef Fajitas

Day 17

Breakfast- Breakfast Cheese Egg Bake

Lunch-Crispy Chicken Wings

Dinner-Lamb Cutlets

Day 18

Breakfast- Spicy Egg Bite

Lunch-Juicy Baked Cod

Dinner-Beef Fajitas

Day 19

Breakfast- Delicious Gruyere Cheese Bacon Egg Bite

Lunch- Delicious Mustard Chicken

Dinner-Garlic Lemon Lamb Chops

Day 20

Breakfast- Healthy Zucchini Frittata

Lunch-Bagel Fish Fillets

Dinner-Creole Chops

Day 21

Breakfast- Cheesy Breakfast Quiche

Lunch-Lemon Garlic Chicken

Dinner-BBQ Pork Chops

Day 22

Breakfast- Breakfast Cheese Egg Bake

Lunch-Tuna Steaks

Dinner-Easy Ranch Pork Chops

Day 23

Breakfast- Herb Egg Muffins

Lunch-Perfect Chicken Tenders

Dinner-Healthy & Juicy Pork Chops

Day 24

Breakfast- Baked Breakfast Donuts

Lunch-Chipotle Shrimp

Dinner-Herb Pork Chops

Day 25

Breakfast- Strawberry Donuts

Lunch-Herb Chicken Wings

Dinner- Tasty Pork Ribs

Day 26

Breakfast- Spicy Egg Bite

Lunch-Shrimp Fajitas

Dinner-Tasty Pork Ribs

Day 27

Breakfast- Delicious Gruyere Cheese Bacon Egg Bite

Lunch-Cajun Chicken

Dinner-Herb Pork Chops

Day 28

Breakfast- Baked Omelet

Lunch-Lemon Garlic Fish

Dinner-Spiced Pork Chops

Day 29

Breakfast- Healthy Zucchini Frittata

Lunch-Spicy Chicken Wings

Dinner-Tasty Pork Ribs

Day 30

Breakfast- Healthy Oatmeal Muffins

Lunch-Horseradish Fish Fillets

Dinner-Spiced Pork Chops

Conclusion

This book was specially designed with the idea of giving you the best hand-picked recipes for your air fryer toaster oven, allowing you to prepare mouthwatering, yet healthy dishes that you can enjoy even on the busiest day of your life. This book can definitely meet your needs! Crispy, effortless and time-saving recipes with this ignited Air Fryer Toaster Oven Cookbook for healthier fried favorites.

So there's only one thing you need to do now is just get one copy of this cookbook and start your cooking tonight!

CPSIA information can be obtained
at www.ICGtesting.com
Printed in the USA
LVHW020522280122
709444LV00007B/335